DON'T SPEND MONEY FOR GENERATING LEADS

A Sales Classic on Lead Generation

SUBRAMANIAN CHANDRAMOULI

INDIA • SINGAPORE • MALAYSIA

Notion Press

No. 8, 3rd Cross Street,
CIT Colony, Mylapore,
Chennai, Tamil Nadu – 600 004

First Published by Notion Press 2021
Copyright © Subramanian Chandramouli 2021
All Rights Reserved.

ISBN 978-1-63781-629-5

This book has been published with all efforts taken to make the material error-free after the consent of the author. However, the author and the publisher do not assume and hereby disclaim any liability to any party for any loss, damage, or disruption caused by errors or omissions, whether such errors or omissions result from negligence, accident, or any other cause.

While every effort has been made to avoid any mistake or omission, this publication is being sold on the condition and understanding that neither the author nor the publishers or printers would be liable in any manner to any person by reason of any mistake or omission in this publication or for any action taken or omitted to be taken or advice rendered or accepted on the basis of this work. For any defect in printing or binding the publishers will be liable only to replace the defective copy by another copy of this work then available.

Contents

Acknowledgements *5*
How Will This Book Be Useful? *7*
Testimonials *9*

1. Oxygen for a Business 17
2. Friends 23
3. Relatives 29
4. Institutions 35
5. Ex-Employers/Employees 41
6. Neighbours 47
7. Doctors-Auditors-Lawyers 53
8. Strangers 59
9. Newspapers and Magazines 65
10. Linkedin 71
11. Youtube Channel 79
12. Seminars and Conferences 85
13. Speaking Assignments 93
14. Testimonials 99
15. Existing Customers 105

Recommended Books for Further Reading *111*
About the Author *113*
Annual Sales Excellence Program *115*

Acknowledgements

I would like to thank my mentors Srinivasan Ranganathan and Meena, Founders of Inside-Out Foundation, for continuously mentoring me. Meeting them was the turning point in my life.

Thanks to my wife, Vidya, who has patiently supported me in all my endeavours.

Thanks to my schoolteachers John Amarnath Sir, Devadoss Sir and Sermugapandiyan Sir. Their timely help in my school days made a big difference in my life.

Photography: Cynthia Sapna Photography

How Will This Book Be Useful?

I have interacted with more than 7500 people who are entrepreneurs or sales executives across 25 different countries. One of the common problems I have noticed with entrepreneurs across countries is generating leads consistently. Irrespective of their business size, many of them face this challenge. When I ask them why they are struggling to generate leads, their answer is they don't have enough money to spend on lead generation.

That's why this book talks about 14 different ways to generate leads without spending any money. In my 10 years as an entrepreneur, I have used all these 14 ways to generate leads for myself. I believe it will be useful for you as well. All these 14 principles will be directly useful for entrepreneurs and sales executives who are in the B2B (Business to Business) segment. For people who are in the B2C (Business to Consumer) segment, some of the 14 ways will be directly applicable and other lead generations ways may be useful for bulk deals. You don't need to follow all 14 ways to generate leads; you can choose ways which align with your natural strengths, and if you focus on that and follow it day in and day out, it will bring a big difference to your business. Wishing you all the very best.

Testimonials

The strength of any business is measured by cashflow—that, in turn, is determined solely by the flow in the pipeline. There's a myth that one needs to spend a lot of money on sales to fill the pipeline. Well! Subbu shows you very clearly why it is just a myth!

Generating leads without spending money, by following simple principles, will provide deep value to anyone who is passionate to succeed as an entrepreneur.

Another hallmark of this book is its amazing readability, very close to being a thrilling novel! Simple and powerful stories are discussed in a typical Indian context, adding much flavour.

This book will surely add immense value to its readers.

Srinivasan Ranganathan, Visiting Professor ISB Hyderabad, India (Mentoring Transformation for Inner Power and Freedom; https://transformentor.in)

Of the numerous books on sales, marketing and lead generation, **DONT SPEND MONEY on Generating LEADS: A Sales Classic on Lead Generation** by Subramanian is truly a remarkable piece. His latest work, a masterpiece for sales experts, instils an immense wealth of knowledge and awareness in the minds of its readers.

Subramanian truly has an amazing way of taking the readers along by sharing his unique experiences and stories. This way, he cultivates a strong sense of imagination and ideation in their minds.

Barely a hundred pages deep, it extensively addresses the emerging trends, surrounding variables and the people around us as the perfect avenues for growth and development. He doesn't stop there; he goes on to encourage critical thinking so readers may be able to relate to his experiences.

The book is a great reminder and roadmap for all entrepreneurs, sales and marketing experts to discover opportunities everywhere. Perhaps, Subramanian does this by immersing the readers so deep into a journey that they learn to recognize and make the best of all that occurs naturally in the day-to-day surroundings. He outlines the steps and procedures required for sales experts to build strong leads and foresee advantages in the future. Indeed, adhering to Subramanian's advice will go a long way!

Zulfiqar Butt, Secretary General (Acting), SAARC Chamber of Commerce, Pakistan

This book speaks directly to the growing breed of entrepreneurs who come either from a tech or a functional background grappling with commercial strategy, especially in the B2B space. Business leaders are typically dealing with a limited budget and rely heavily on their personal network. This book provides a structured process and a practical toolkit to help generate leads in these situations. Subbu has crystallized his years of sales experience "pounding the pavement" and packed it into this simple, lucid book. Must read!!

Balki G. Iyer, Chief Commercial Officer, Eos Energy Storage, United States

Leads are at the top of the sales funnel for every business. Inadequate quantity and quality of leads will cascade to a poor sales cycle. This might eventually affect the overall business model. Hence, it is imperative for every entrepreneur and hence sales executives to focus on leads with utmost importance.

Subbu helps entrepreneurs understand the importance of lead generation and also provides step by step ways and methods to generate leads, starting with **personal network** & **personal actions**. It is very impressive that each chapter has a scenario and story(ies) to help readers understand the context and deliberate on their own individual situations. This book is a must for every first-time entrepreneur and sales executives.

Saravana Mani, Head - Open Innovation Kmart, Author of the book *Open Innovation Playbook*, **India**

This book is more of implementable ideas than theory. Stories make it easier to understand the concepts. Step by step approach to each concept will help entrepreneurs and small business owners to easily implement the learnings. This is a highly recommended book to all who want to continuously generate leads without spending any money.

Dr. Parimal Merchant, Director, Global Family Managed Business Program, SP Jain School of Global Management

It's a must-read book for any entrepreneur who is thinking big. If you are planning to turn your ideas into a profitable company, this book is for you. As an entrepreneur and entrepreneurship teacher, I would say this book contains all the information any startup needs that is usually not explained in college. You don't have to reinvent the wheel—*DONT*

SPEND MONEY on Generating LEADS helps to avoid common mistakes and shows shortcuts to success.

Dr. Arturas Jurgelevicius, Startup Consultant, Lithuania

Lead generation is a very crucial first step in the sales process. The lead base provides a good foundation in achieving sales success stories. As I go through this book, it is suggested to be a handbook of any budding salespeople and smart startups. The stories articulate the points to be in our minds as we go about daily sales chores. Subramanian also guides us in removing the inhibitions and notions we may have in bringing about the best salesperson. Overall, it is a must-read for all startups/salespeople to populate the leads and achieve sales success. Now that the reader has the book in hand, waste no time in going through these chapters and creating value for the business.

Hari Balasubramanian, Business Development Director, Janitza Electronics, Dubai

Each one of us, irrespective of the profession, will be able to relate, understand and apply the key concepts shared in this book in our everyday lives. The author provides a paradigm shift to the conventional lead generation concepts and makes it extremely simple, yet effective through analogies, stories and powerful examples. This is a highly recommended book to read and practice.

Rajanikanth K, Leadership Expert, Author of the book *Magical Presentations*, **India**

I have known Subbu for many years and he has played a pivotal role in shaping many sales professionals by imparting top-level training programs. He has lived his journey on one key aspect of sales—"Lead Generation"—through this book. Being in this profession for decades, I must say that his journey written through this book is a must-have for every organization that wants to build a classy sales bunch of folks.

The basic kick off in sales happens to be the toughest, which is lead generation. It's challenging, it's pressurizing at times and for those who want to breathe easy, get this copy now. One can't have such detailing in simplified terms which is penned down with learnings from real life. I was amazed by such fantastic dealing by Subbu.

Get a copy and you can get on your sales journey with so much confidence. That's something which you can be assured of.

Danan Christadoss, Country Head, redBus, Indonesia

Building your sales pipeline with quality leads and without spending money is a very core skill and no one better than Subbu (as he is fondly known) to explain this key concept in a concise, entertaining and easy to follow template. Invaluable knowledge for everyone who needs to know about sales, growth, steady cashflows. Worth reading again and again. Great book.

Vijetha Shastry, Executive Director, TiE Bangalore, India

Subramanian has an uncanny knack for delivering complex concepts in a simple palatable way. His third book, *Don't Spend Money on Generating Leads: A Sales Classic on Lead Generation*, is a must-read for all startups who are striving to predictably generate quality leads.

Peppered with real stories (relatable too) and coupled with practical and easily implementable ideas, this book will be one of my strong recommendations to global startups, small businesses and wannabe entrepreneurs.

Rama Iyer, Head - Innovation (Airports) @ GMR Group, Author of the book *Innovation Ecosystem in India*, **Hyderabad, India**

Leads are the most important aspects in sales and, if done the right way, can help companies strengthen their pipeline and increase cash flow. This book clearly identifies the various ways to create leads and explains the step by step approach to help create leads through simple means.

I would encourage entrepreneurs, people in their early career in sales/BD to read this book to prepare themselves and for experienced sales leaders, a great reminder to refresh as well.

Subramanian has a knack for using powerful stories to put the point across and hit us hard on why doing small things brings great benefits.

Venkata Krishnan, Executive Director, Country Manager India, Utopus Insights

The best sales are to make customers think that you are always next to them and always waiting for them like a friend. It's a book that tells you how to do it.

Yoon Kim, Founder of StarFeed.com, South Korea

Being an effective hustler and sales expert requires heart and perseverance. For that, one needs to follow a disciplined lead generation strategy. In *Don't Spend Money on Generating Leads: A Sales Classic on Lead Generation* by Subramanian, you will get hands-on, executable insights into how to build a quality pipeline and reach the sales goals you always wished for, while building long-lasting client relationships with heart. Subbu has helped many of our German and European startup entrepreneurs build a pipeline with Indian clients and turn leads into business, and so can you. A must-read for first-time entrepreneurs and startup founders.

Juliane Frömmter, Program Lead, EU-India InnoCenter, Germany

Having spent close to 2 decades as a rainmaker across various industries and markets, more so in setting up new territories and rolling out new services/products, I can relate to the context of how leads are the "Oxygen for Business." Generating meaningful leads which convert to business is more about the process than the past laurels. You have to always start from zero; you have to always follow the process. This book unlike others is less talk and more action. Borrowed from life experiences, it states those do's and don'ts which make it an absolute must-read for sales folks across experience bands.

Suman Mishra, CTO, 3ev Industries, India

Lead generation is a continuous process and has been aptly emphasized by Subramanian in this book. Sales leaders and startup founders can easily build a customized framework using the techniques mentioned in this book. I can confidently suggest that it should be a handbook on lead generation for all wannabe entrepreneurs and all startup founders.

Saikiran J. Vedula, Head of Inward Investment, Department for International Trade, UK

1

Oxygen for a Business

Krishna runs a web design company. He designs and builds websites for small businesses and solopreneurs. Generally, he builds 5 to 6 websites in a month, and he employs 4 people to support him. He wants to build at least 9 to 10 websites in a month to be profitable and have enough positive cash flow. He knows he has enough bandwidth to do that. But he is not able to generate enough leads to achieve the desired revenue.

Krishna lives in Bangalore, India, and an unverified report says there are more than 100,000 entrepreneurs in Bangalore, which includes small businesses, startups and solopreneurs. Krishna's target is just 10 websites per month, and today every business needs a website. Being a website building company, he can get clients from anywhere in the world. When the market is very huge, why is Krishna struggling to get business? One of the reasons is, he doesn't have a lead generation process which can give him leads whenever he wants. Leads won't come to you automatically; you have to work to get leads consistently. In other words, there should be a system which generates leads consistently.

There are 4 reasons why lead generation is an important aspect of a business, and that's why I call it the *oxygen for a business*. Once Krishna understands the below 4 reasons, he will spend more time on lead generation and will also create a lead generation process.

No Leads, No Sales

No leads, no sales. It may look like a simple statement and you may feel like you know this very well. Knowing is different, doing is different. As an entrepreneur, every day you have thousands of problems to face and you forget to think about lead generation as it doesn't give you immediate results. Any lead generated today will give you money after 1 week, 1 month, 6 months or even 1 year, based on the product or service you sell. And hence, you don't feel the importance of it and may spend more time on something which gives you money today for your survival. But smart businesspersons and salespeople understand that if they don't spend time today in generating leads, tomorrow they will not have anything to work on.

Fewer Leads, Less Work for Your Employees

Being an entrepreneur myself—and once upon a time I had 25 employees in my company—my biggest problem was to have continuous work for all my employees all the time. Sometimes we have too much work when employees have to stretch and work, and sometimes we do not have enough work for all the employees. The problem is we don't have enough leads all the time. I was running an e-learning company and each project would take 2 to 3 weeks to complete. Imagine, if I have 10 quality leads per week and 5 right prospects out of it every week, I will never go out of work. But just like many entrepreneurs, I also made the mistake of focusing too much on delivery (which I should have delegated) and spent little time on lead generation. All the profit you made in a successful delivery get drained out if your employees don't have enough work for just 1 week. It's very important to have consistent work for all your employees and maintain 90% plus employee utilization if you are a startup or small business. To achieve this, you should have enough quality leads which flow in consistently.

Fewer Leads, Wrong Prospects

Prospect, in simple terms, is someone who is a potential customer. It is very important for a salesperson and entrepreneur to evaluate whether a lead is a right prospect or not. Choosing the right prospect has many criteria, and the most important one is whether the prospect has money, the authority to buy and compelling need to buy your product or service. You can have the luxury of choosing the right prospect only when you have enough leads. If you got only 4 leads in the last one month, then you have to pursue all 4 leads. You may finally end up with closing most probably zero or, in the best case, 1 deal out of that 4. Instead, if you got 40 leads in the last one month, you can choose the right prospect out of that 40, which may be 10 or 12, and you will most probably close 3 or 4 deals out of it. That too with the prospect with whom you want to do business. Not having enough leads will force us to choose the wrong prospects, which in turn will waste our time and money. Most importantly, we will lose our peace of mind.

More Leads, Better Price

The number of leads you have in your pipeline decides your ability to negotiate. As we discussed in the above example, when you have only 4 leads in a month, how much confidence will you have in negotiation? You are desperate to win the project, as you have to give work to your employees. So, you end up signing the project with little profit, which becomes negative if there are any project overruns. But if you have 40 leads, you price for profit and if the prospect asks for a price below your walk-away price, you can walk away without any fear. This is because you have more leads to work on and winning 3 deals in a month is more than sufficient to cover your cost. I recommend you read my book *Sales for Startups* to understand more about *quoted price* and *walk-away price*. When you have more leads, it gives you the freedom to price better and negotiate better.

As we have now understood that leads are the oxygen for any business, in the following chapters of this book we will discuss 14 different ways to generate leads without spending any money.

Key Takeaways

- Lead generation is the oxygen for any business
- When there are no leads, there are no sales. You need to have a consistent lead generation system
- When there are fewer leads, there is less work for employees. Hence, you cannot get the maximum productivity from your employees
- When there are fewer leads, you tend to work with the wrong prospects. You lose the freedom to choose the right prospect
- When there are more leads, you have the freedom to price better and negotiate better with your prospects

QUESTIONS TO PONDER

Do you have a system which gives you leads consistently?

_____

_____

_____

How many leads have you generated in the last month?

_____

_____

_____

List down the sources which generate leads for you.

_____

_____

_____

Lead generation is the oxygen for business. Having a system for continuous lead generation will give you peace of mind and the power to choose your clients.

2

Friends

Aniruddh was living in Dubai for the past 20 years. He was working for a big retail firm in Dubai in their supply chain division. He is a native of Kerala, a southern state in India. He decided to come back to his state once and for all. He is in his mid-forties and wants to work for another 12 to 15 years. He decided to start his own retail consulting firm as he is a domain expert. He decided to settle in Cochin, the most prominent city of Kerala.

In another 15 days, he is going to start the 2nd innings of his life. He is very anxious and tensed as he doesn't know whether he will survive as an entrepreneur. He has 3 close childhood friends in Cochin. He had a video chat with them and asked for their help to connect with IT companies who are in the retail domain or to connect with upcoming retail chains in Kerala. To his surprise, when he landed in Cochin, his friends had already set up 3 meetings for him, 2 with IT retail product companies and one with a growing supermarket brand. In the next month, he closed 2 retainership deals as a consultant with one IT company and with the supermarket brand.

What Aniruddh did smartly was to talk to his friends, whom he has known for the last 35+ years, much before he reached Kerala and that gave his friends enough time to get leads for him. Trust is already built, and his friends will take sincere efforts to really help him. That's the power of friendship. A friend will never get angry when you ask for her/his help. Actually, they will be happy to help you. That's why in my

FRIENDS framework of lead generation, the first letter F stands for friends. As a startup entrepreneur or small business owner, you have to leverage your friends and ask for help. Of course, you can also help them in any possible way. Giving is a two-way activity.

5-step Process to Generate Leads Through Your Friends

Step 1: Create a list

Create a list of friends from whom you can ask for help. Generally, on the first level, we have 2 or 3 friends we call our very close friends. At the second level, we may have around 25 to 30 friends who are close to us. I recommend using this 2nd level of friend circle and creating a list of friends. Put it in an Excel sheet. If you don't have contact details for them, work on it. Be ready with the list. These are the people you are ready to help any day.

Step 2: Specific ask

The next step is to have clarity on what help you need. If you use confusing statements like "I need business connections, can you help?", "I want to grow my business. How can you help me?"—such statements will confuse your friend and he/she would not know how to help you. You should be clear and specific in your ask. In the above example, Aniruddh was very clear in his ask: to connect him to the founders of IT companies who are in the retail space or the owner of upcoming supermarkets. This gives clarity to his friends. Only when people have clarity, they can help you. If you ask them to find clarity for you and then help, most probably you will not get any help. Make it easy for the other person to help you. Be very clear in your ask. Use a brand name which will trigger many more names in your friend's mind. Say, for example, can you connect me to the procurement manager of Bata or companies like Bata? This question will make your friend get you a connection for Bata or Adidas or Nike or Puma. Specific is terrific.

Step 3: Take the action: call

Now you are ready with the list and clear about what you want. It's time to take action. Pick up the phone and make a call. After your general discussion, go for that specific ask. Our general discussions depend on our age. In our teenage, we discuss film stars or sportspersons; in middle age, we discuss real estate, financial planning, our kids; in older age, we discuss health and retirement. Whatever your general discussion is, after that discussion, without any hesitation, ask for that specific introduction to your potential customer.

Step 4: Follow up

People may genuinely want to help you, but because of their day-to-day firefighting, they forget things. It's your job to remind your friend about your ask. Once a week, you can send her a gentle reminder. Trust me, your friend will not mistake you for that. It's you who assumes what she will think. She will not think anything wrong. Actually, she doesn't have time to think about you, that's why she forgot to help in the first place. So, just send a gentle reminder. For more details about how to follow up, I recommend you read my first book *Anybody Can Sell*, which has a dedicated chapter on follow-ups.

Step 5: Don't expect immediate results

In lead generation, we need to have patience. You are asking 10 or 20 of your friends for help. First, don't expect results from all of them. Only 1 or 2 are going to give you that referral. It's ok. Even they may not do it immediately. It may happen after the 7th or 8th follow-up. But that 1 or 2 referrals may give you huge revenue. Your job is to keep asking and following up. Results will definitely come, but you don't know when they will come. Patience is of the utmost importance in the FRIENDS framework. That connection with the procurement head of Bata may happen after 8 months, when your friend's sister joins Bata as the procurement head. We never know what the future has in store for us.

Key Takeaways

- In the FRIENDS framework, the first letter F stands for friends
- To get results, you have to follow the 5-step process
- Step 1 is to create a list of friends you can ask for help
- Step 2 is to have clarity on what is your specific ask
- Step 3 is to take action. That is to call your friend over the phone
- Step 4 is to follow up again and again at regular intervals
- Step 5 is to have patience and not to expect immediate results

QUESTIONS TO PONDER

Who are your friends from whom you can ask for help?
_____
_____
_____

What is the specific reference you want to ask your friend?
_____
_____
_____

What is the frequency of follow-up you are comfortable with?
_____
_____
_____

> When you ask your friend for help, they will help you without any expectation. Life will definitely give you an opportunity to help them in return. Do not feel shy to ask for help.

3

Relatives

Kunal is 30 years old and just started his recruitment consultancy firm. He has 2 sisters, and they have a very close relationship. He also knows that a woman loves her brother the most, next to their father, and that makes the brother-in-law relationship very special. His brother-in-law is working as an HR head in a manufacturing company. He asked his brother-in-law to give him just one lead whom he can meet and pitch to for his business.

Kunal is good in sales and very diligent in his follow-ups. His brother-in-law connected him to his ex-boss, who is now heading HR for a large European manufacturing company. Kunal called him and sought an appointment. In the meeting, the HR head asked Kunal why he should give him a chance when he already has 15 vendors working as recruitment partners. Kunal thought for a moment and asked if there is any current open position which is not filled by these 15 vendors. The HR head thought for a moment and said that they need a specialist painter, which they have not been able to find for the last 9 months. Kunal made a deal with the HR head that if he closes this position, he should be inducted as a vendor for this company.

For the next 2 months, Kunal and his team travelled to many tier 2 cities in India, conducted tests and found some good candidates. Not one but 5 painters joined the company within the next 3 months. As promised, he became the vendor for the European company and soon he became the most preferred recruitment partner for that company.

Many of us can work hard and work smart like Kunal, but we need a brother-in-law to make that introduction. The point to note here is Kunal is able to **ask** his relative for a lead.

The moment we are born on this earth, we already have 2 relatives—our parents. Then our parents have their siblings and their kids. Easily, all of us have 25+ relatives. After marriage, the number of relatives doubles to 50. Some of you may not be comfortable to ask some of your relatives for a lead. Remove those 10 to 15% of relatives with whom you are not comfortable, you will still have 40+ people from whom you can ask for a connection. They all are working in a company or running a company. Are you leveraging your relationship with them? In the above example, Kunal was able to leverage his brother-in-law and that gave him a good start on his entrepreneurial journey. Below are the steps which will help you leverage to get connections from your relatives.

Step 1

Open an Excel sheet or a notebook and write down the names of all your relatives. Take the help of your spouse so that you don't miss any of them. Then in the next column, write down where they work and what position they hold. If you don't know what their role is, note it down to ask them this question. I am sure you will have a list of 30 to 40 people now. Now remove the people with whom you are not comfortable. You would have got a list of at least 25 people.

Step 2

On a weekend, call these 25 people. If they are in the same town, go and meet them in person. Request them to connect you to just one person who can be your prospective customer. It can be in the same company they work for or through their contacts any one company where you can go and meet the decision-maker. Don't ask for business. It scares them. Ask only for a connection. Remember to follow up diligently if they ask for time to work on it. When I started my company in the year

2010, I created a similar list and asked my relatives for 2 connections. Before I completed 60% of the list, I had enough prospects to meet and didn't get a chance to complete the remaining part of the list. There wasn't a need.

Step 3

Just like Kunal, take action, give a compelling offer which is a win-win for the prospect and you and bring the deal to closure. Any lead which is worth being closed should be closed. You should not miss it because of your lack of follow up.

Step 4

This step is very important. Once you complete the transaction and receive the money, thank your relative who gave you that lead. Every year, you will have at least one family function where you will meet all your relatives. When you are having a chat with a group of your relatives, appreciate the person who gave you that lead in front of everybody. Be genuine and lavish in your words. ***Any action which is respected, recognized and rewarded will be repeated.*** It's not about giving expensive gifts to them. They are not looking for that. The intent of showing gratitude is more important. Here, emotional value has higher weightage than economical value. This appreciation will motivate him/her to give you more connections and, more importantly, other people who are listening to this will start giving you leads.

In my first 2 years of entrepreneurship, I did not ask my wife for leads. Then one fine day, I requested 30 minutes of her time and asked for specific leads. My wife is good at networking. She spoke to many of her classmates and, within the next month, she connected me to 7 people who can be my potential customers. Finally, I started doing business with 2 of them. Sometimes we miss out on asking people who are so close to us. For every entrepreneur or salesperson, there is a good number of leads within their family. All you have to do is come out of this inhibition of *what will people think if I ask for help?* Fact is, nobody has time to think about you. If you strongly believe that you are doing good to your customer, you are solving his/her problem and helping your customer in their business, then don't be shy to ask for connections. Even to do good, you have to ask.

Key Takeaways

- In the FRIENDS framework, the second letter R stands for relatives
- To get better results, follow the 4-step process
- Step 1 is to create a list of relatives you can ask for help
- Step 2 is to meet them or call them and ask for connections
- Step 3 is to take action. Convert the leads to closure
- Step 4 is to appreciate them in front of other relatives. Be genuine and lavish in your words

QUESTIONS TO PONDER

Who are your relatives in senior positions in the industry?
_____
_____
_____

Who are the first 5 people among your relatives you are going to meet and ask for connections?
_____
_____
_____

When you close deals from the leads given by your relatives, how will you show your gratitude?
_____
_____
_____

> People spend huge money to generate leads but forget to leverage the connections of their own family members.

4

Institutions

Anish is an industrial design expert. He has worked for the past 20 years in the industry and created some stunning designs. He started his own design firm recently. He thought because of his existing contacts and his reputation in the field, he will easily get business. Six months have passed by after his entrepreneurial debut, but he is yet to get any big breakthrough. He got some small orders, but it is not enough to take care of his monthly expenses.

Anish met his uncle Arijit, who is a business consultant. He spoke to him about his problem of not getting enough business. Arijit asked him whether he is leveraging his school and college contacts. Suddenly, a thought struck Anish that so many of his classmates are currently working in senior positions in the industry. Anish did his under graduation in design from a very reputed college in Bangalore and did his master's in industrial design from India's most reputed design school in Ahmedabad. He started calling his classmates, mailing them one by one, and within 3 months, he got a very big order which will take 9 months of execution. From then on, he understood the most powerful way of generating leads: leveraging your connections from the institutions you studied. Leveraging his classmates has become an important lead generation activity for Anish.

Every one of us studied in a school, went to a college and some of us have done a master's program. Many of us went to tuitions, a foreign language course or a sports course or even arts. We have spent time in multiple institutions. We have spent time with many people in our life. We may have maintained contact with some of them. If not, it's not very tough to find out where they are now. We can leverage Facebook, LinkedIn or Instagram to find them out. Anish was able to find most of his classmates through LinkedIn.

As an entrepreneur or salesperson, leveraging your contacts from the institution you studied is one of the effective ways to generate leads. Especially in B2B leads, all you need is a connection to get an appointment, and once you get an appointment, it is all about communicating the value you can add to your prospect, following up and closing the sale.

When I started my first recruitment company in December 2010, this is how I got my first client.

3rd Friday of December 2010 was my last working day as a sales manager in one of the top software services company in India. The following Monday was going to be my first working day as an entrepreneur. That Friday night, after my send-off party in the software company, I reached home late. But already my mind started thinking about what I would do from Monday as an entrepreneur. That Friday night, I took my laptop and gathered the contact details of all my 98 classmates from my MBA batch. I studied Global MBA from SP Jain School of Global Management-Dubai, Singapore. I had a very good relationship with all of my 98 batchmates.

I wrote a mail to all 98 of them, announcing my first step to entrepreneurship, and asked them for help in connecting to me companies who need recruitment services. The next morning when I opened my mail, there were many congratulatory messages and there was one important mail from my MBA classmate and friend *Chetan Bafna*. He congratulated me and asked me to work on 8 positions for the new e-commerce venture he was just starting in Mumbai. I called him immediately and asked for more details, and we finalized the commercials. Within the next 2 months, I received my 1st cheque as an entrepreneur from my friend and classmate Chetan Bafna. He is a serial entrepreneur and is currently running a real estate software firm called *Lockated* in Mumbai. Even though I was new to the recruitment industry, my friend Chetan had trust in me. Monday morning when I started my entrepreneurial journey, I already had a paying customer who is my friend and classmate. That's the power of the relationships you build in the institutions you studied. Within the next year, many of my classmates started referring me to their contacts and even today my classmates are of great help in my business.

Steps to Leverage Your Classmates

Open an Excel sheet and start writing the names of the classmates you remember from school, college, post-graduation or any other institute you studied in. Then go to LinkedIn and find out where they are currently working. Identify who can help you in your lead generation and make a note in the Excel sheet. Mail them or call them and ask for a meeting; it can be face to face or a video meeting. Talk to them and ask for help. Follow up and get the leads. It is as simple as that. Most of you will have WhatsApp groups with school mates and college mates. Leverage that. Don't feel shy to ask for help in getting a connection to the company they are working in or any other connections they can give. You also offer help in the group. What goes around comes around. As an entrepreneur and salesperson, you may have many contacts. Help your classmates with your contacts. Then, you will not feel bad when you ask for help. You cannot run a business only with your own contacts. This life is full of interdependence and lead generation is all about helping others and accepting help from others.

Key Takeaways

- Institution refers to schools, colleges, tuition centres, art classes, foreign language course centres, sports centres or wherever you have spent time in your life and built relationships with people

- Create a list of all the institutions you are a part of and write down the names of the classmates you remember
- Go to LinkedIn and connect with them
- Once connected on LinkedIn, meet them in person or through video conference
- Offer them help wherever you can and ask for help
- Ask them about other classmates' contact details and get connected with them
- Keep doing this continuously and generate leads

QUESTIONS TO PONDER

What are the institutions you are a part of?
___
___
___

Who are the classmates you are comfortable with to ask for help?
___
___
___

How many leads can you generate in a month from your institution classmates?
___
___
___

> The best time in life is spent in the institution you studied and wonderful relationships you built. Offer help to your classmates and don't be shy in taking help from them.

5

Ex-Employers/Employees

Gokul is an entrepreneur who runs an e-learning company. He is struggling to generate leads and thinking of how to improve his sales pipeline. He has worked in 3 different software companies before starting his own company. He browsed through LinkedIn and started looking through where all his ex-colleagues are currently working. He saw that one of his ex-colleagues, Madhav, has just joined one of the world's largest education company.

Ten years back, Gokul and Madhav worked together in a startup product company. That startup company was very employee-friendly and whenever there was a cricket match happening, all the people used to discuss the cricket scores. Gokul and Madhav became friends as both of them are very fond of cricket. Even though they worked in different teams, they watched cricket matches in the cafeteria on a big screen and discussed cricket. Gokul last spoke to Madhav 2 years back. When Gokul saw Madhav joined this Fortune 1000 education company through LinkedIn, he just called him. After an initial exchange about their recent sports craze, Madhav asked Gokul how his company is growing. Gokul updated him about his latest clients and the projects that are going on. Then Madhav asked him whether he would be interested to work with his current organization as they are looking for new partners for their dream project. Gokul was elated and happily accepted the help. Madhav connected him to their content head and with further meetings and continuous follow-ups, in a matter of 9 months, Gokul's company signed a contract with that Fortune 1000 company. They are now one of the 4 partners across Asia who create e-learning content for this multi-billion-dollar company.

Gokul was lucky; without even asking for that connection, Madhav connected him. The credit also goes to Gokul, as he took the effort of scanning his ex-colleagues on LinkedIn and reaching out to them. If you are an entrepreneur or salesperson, there is a high chance that you would have worked in 2 or 3 companies before starting your company or working in your current company. You have already built many relationships in your working career. Are you leveraging that relationship? Your ex-colleagues may now work in different companies who can be your prospective customers. Talk to them and ask for a connection. Every week, if you just talk to 2 of your ex-colleagues, you would reach 104 people in a year, and if 10% of them connects their current company to you, you have 10 clients who are interested to listen to you. You can convert 2 or 3 customers out of it. It will take hardly 10 minutes a week to talk to your ex-colleagues. You have already invested a huge amount of time in building that relationship when you worked with that person in the past. Now, leverage that connection for your business. Of course, you can also offer help to your ex-colleagues in whichever way they need help. As an entrepreneur, you have a better network and you can help your ex-colleague with your connections. It's a two-way channel. Help others and be ready to receive help. Many people are ready to help others but don't have the mindset to seek help.

Employees

If you are an entrepreneur, leverage the connections of your employees. Many entrepreneurs think only their salespeople have to generate leads. When I was running my e-learning company, I announced a scheme to all my employees, which included software engineers, recruiters, test engineers, designers, to come with connections from their past employment. They would connect me to their colleagues from the previous companies they worked with. I would talk to them and get a meeting with the right person in that company. When I closed a deal, I would give gift vouchers to my employees and appreciate them for their contribution. Every year, I got at least 3-4 customers in this way. You have to leverage not only your ex-colleagues but also the ex-colleagues of your employees.

Steps involved in leveraging connections of ex-employers/employees

1. Create a list of your ex-colleagues. You can easily get 25 to 30 names
2. Go to LinkedIn and see where they are currently working
3. Whichever company can be your prospective customers, talk to those ex-colleagues
4. Ask them to connect you to the relevant person in their company
5. Follow up continuously, get a meeting, send a proposal and close the deal
6. Announce a referral scheme to all your employees
7. Get connected to their ex-colleagues and repeat steps 4 and 5

If you keep this as a process you do every 6 months, you are sure to get 2-3 good customers every year.

Another suggestion is you can also reach out to the founder of your past employer and ask for a meeting. That company itself may be a prospective customer for you. The entrepreneur of that company would be happy to give work to one of his/her ex-colleagues, provided you give value to him/her. Entrepreneurs help each other. Take that first step in reaching out to your past employer.

Key Takeaways

- Leverage the connections of your ex-colleagues as they may now work in a new company
- Find out through LinkedIn and connect with them

- Seek out help and ask for connections
- Get connected, meet them, send a proposal and win the deal
- If you are an entrepreneur, announce a referral scheme to all your employees
- Leverage their connections to their ex-colleagues

QUESTIONS TO PONDER

How many ex-colleagues are you in touch with?
___
___
___

Do you know where your ex-colleagues are currently working?
___
___
___

Is your past employer a prospective customer to you?
___
___
___

> Your ex-colleagues know your strength and trust you. Connect with them and seek their help.

6

Neighbours

Nilesh runs a recruitment firm. He has been in this business for the past 2 years. He booked a 3-bedroom flat a year back, and he just shifted to his new apartment. His apartment complex has 84 flats. He interacted with his neighbours and within 2 months he understood that most of the people in his apartment complex work in IT or BPO companies, which are his target customers. He is yet to make friends with his apartment people. Also, in most of the houses, both men and women go to work, which means more possible customers for Nilesh.

Nilesh loves to play cricket. One day, he sent a message to his apartment WhatsApp group regarding forming a cricket club within the apartment. With his own money, he bought cricket kits and asked who can join him over the weekend to play cricket. The first week, a few people joined and then the gang grew every week. After a few months, there are 60 people in his cricket WhatsApp group, and half of them are not even from his apartment because many people introduced their colleagues who live in the same area and want to join the cricket team. One day, after the cricket match during the weekend, when everybody was having tea and snacks, Nilesh spoke about his recruitment company and asked if anybody has any hiring requirement. One of the players, Mahesh, said he wants to hire data science engineers for his team. Nilesh asked him to connect him with the HR person of his company who is responsible for hiring. Mahesh smiled and introduced Ashok, who was standing next to him and is also a part of the cricket team. Nilesh never knew Ashok is responsible for hiring. Within the next 6 months, Nilesh did a business of 1 million Indian rupees with Mahesh's company.

Many entrepreneurs and salespeople don't leverage their neighbours. In today's world, most of you live in apartment complexes. Many people live around you. They all work in a company which can be your prospective customer. And you meet your neighbours day in and day out. Without spending any money, you have an opportunity to generate leads. Nilesh was smart enough to leverage this and got a good client through his neighbour.

Below are the steps to generate leads from your apartment community.

Be Visible

If your apartment has 100s of units, people may not know you automatically. You have to put in extra efforts to make yourself visible. In the above story, Nilesh made himself visible by creating a cricket group. You can also create a group based on your natural interest. It can be sports, cultural, art or whatever you are interested in. You take initiative to create it and take care that you meet all the members periodically, say once a week or once in 15 days. This way you get to interact with many people, and they will remember you. Every apartment will have a welfare association, you can take leadership roles or be a committee member so that you are known to many people in your apartment community. I used to participate in solo dance and group dance in our apartment's new year party. This particular event has connected me to many people, and we have become friends.

Make Them Experience Your Product or Service

The best way to get a lead from your neighbours is to make them experience your product or service. If your business is into something which they can experience themselves, it is great. Like, if you are running an art studio, you can conduct a competition for kids in the apartment. If you run a business which is based on any particular skill, then conduct a free session. Say you run a software company with emerging technologies, you can conduct a session on analytics or artificial intelligence or blockchain and ask interested people to join the session. Promote this in your apartment WhatsApp group so that everybody knows what you are doing.

Create a Close Circle

You may not make friends with everybody, but at least have a close circle within your apartment complex. If your complex has 100 units, at least you should have 10 people who know you well. They can start giving you leads, and then they can connect you to their close circle in the apartment. They will do this once you fulfil their leads to closure and get a good testimonial from that customer.

Be in Their Mind

Out of mind is out of sight. Once in 15 days or at least once a month, keep reminding them about your company and your services. You can create flyers or videos and post them in WhatsApp groups. Keep contributing to the welfare of your apartment complex in whatever way possible. Talk to people when you meet them in the corridor or the car park. Make conversations in the lift with whoever you are travelling with. It doesn't need to be a business conversation. Spend more time on making yourself visible. Business leads will follow automatically.

Know Them Well

Once you get connected to many people within your apartment complex, do some research and understand where they work. Explore whether their current company can be your potential customer or not. If yes, then politely ask them whether they can connect you to the relevant person in their company. Don't ask them for business; ask them only for a connection. Give them enough reasons as to why you are good in your domain and how it will add value to their company. Don't force them. If they show interest in connecting you, follow up with them. They may forget after a few days. It is your duty to politely follow up and get that connection.

Have Gratitude

Once you get leads and make it to closure, thank them well. Thank them in public, thank them in the WhatsApp group. Be genuine and lavish in your gratitude. This will encourage others to give you leads. People like to help successful people. It is important that whatever leads you get, you take it to business closure. If you are not living in an apartment or villa complex and instead live in an individual house, you can implement the above points in your locality's welfare association.

Key Takeaways

- Neighbours can give you good leads
- Be visible in your apartment/villa complex
- Create events/opportunities to make your neighbours experience your product/service
- Have a close circle within your apartment complex who can help you generate leads
- Be in their mind. Periodically remind them about your product/service
- You should know your neighbours well. Do research and understand where they work, what they do
- Do follow up and take the leads to closure

QUESTIONS TO PONDER

How many people in your apartment know you well?
_____
_____
_____

How many people in your apartment work in a company which can be your prospective client?
_____
_____
_____

What are the actions you are going to take to make yourself visible in your apartment complex?
_____
_____
_____

> Without spending any extra money, you can generate many leads from your living community. Leverage it to the maximum.

7

Doctors-Auditors-Lawyers

Brijesh is running a company which is into IT networking. He sets up IT infrastructure whenever a company expands its office and/or starts operation in a new building. Due to the pandemic, he was struggling to get new orders. One day, he got a mail from his auditor regarding the annual filing of tax returns, and suddenly he got an idea. He requested his auditor for a meeting. He met with his auditor, explained his current situation and requested him to connect him with some of his customers. His auditor referred him to 3 of his multinational clients who are in expansion mode. Brijesh got a business of 7 million Indian rupees from 1 of those 3 clients.

Many entrepreneurs are not as smart as Brijesh. They don't take help from the person they trust. In order to fulfil the FRIENDS framework, D stands for Doctors. Actually, what I mean is doctors, auditors, lawyers, architects and all other professionals. As a businessman or a salesperson, you will come across many professionals and all of them can give you a lot of leads. Just like Brijesh, if you take help from your doctors, auditors, lawyers and architects, you can generate more leads.

For the past 16 years, for my throat infection, I have been visiting the same doctor near my locality. She is very good, and with her prescription, I get cured within 3 days. After understanding the FRIENDS framework, one day when I met my doctor, I asked her whether she can refer me to some of her business clients. She said yes, but being a busy doctor, she forgot to connect. I followed up with her on all Sundays for the next few weeks, as she is free only on Sunday. Within a month, she connected me to one of her contacts, who works as the HR head in a billion-dollar company. I spoke to that HR head, met him and gave a proposal for sales training. Doctors have a lot of connections, and generally, we go to the same doctor and build a relationship. There is nothing wrong with asking them for a business connection. Think about your relationship with your auditor—you trust him and share all your financial information. He/she is not only working for you, but he/she will also have 100+ clients and many of them can be your prospective customers. You request your auditor to give an introduction; don't ask him for business. If he connects you to at least 10 of his customers, it is a very good lead generation activity for you.

The same goes for lawyers and architects. They have a lot of business contacts. Their job is to meet new people every day. They can be an amazing lead source for you. People have inhibitions to ask. When I ask my training participants whether they are comfortable to ask for business connections from their doctors, many of them said, "It is not right to ask for business connections from a doctor." According to me, it is not wrong to ask for a connection from a doctor who you have been visiting for many years. Trust is already built; the doctor will be ready to connect you. She will not have any problem. It is the entrepreneur who has the inhibition to ask. What can be the worst outcome? You may not get a business connection. That's all. It will not affect the relationship you have built for many years.

Steps Involved in Generating Leads from Professionals

Step 1: Write down a list of auditors, lawyers, architects, doctors you know

Step 2: Ask for an appointment with them

Step 3: Meet them and ask for connections to businesspeople or senior corporate executives

Step 4: Follow up till you get connections

Step 5: Meet those connections and bring it to business closure

Step 6: Thank your auditor, lawyer, doctor, architect for their connections and update them that you have closed business

Step 7: Repeat all the above 6 steps at least once a year

Many a time, leads are around us. All we have to do is look around, observe and leverage. When you meet auditors, lawyers, doctors, architects, offer them help as well. Tell them you have a lot of business connections, and for their personal work, if they need any connection, you can help them. This way, you will feel happy to help those professionals and you will not feel bad that you are taking help from them. As an entrepreneur and salesperson, you should have both a giving and receiving attitude. I see that many people are ready to give but not willing to receive anything from others. If you don't have the attitude to receive, the world will not give it to you. Entrepreneurs should work on both a giving and receiving attitude to excel in lead generation. Being biased to any one attitude will affect the other attitude.

Key Takeaways

- It is important to ask for business connections from the people you have already built trust with
- Your auditor has many customers who can be your customers as well
- Doctors have many patients who are senior executives or businesspeople
- Lawyers and architects also have a lot of business connections
- Meet these professionals once in 6 months or once a year and ask for business connections
- Follow up diligently
- Bring those connections to closure
- Thank your auditor, lawyer, doctor, architect once you close the business

QUESTIONS TO PONDER

Do you have a list of all the auditors, lawyers, doctors, architects you know?

_____
_____
_____

When was the last time you asked for a business connection from your auditor?

_____
_____
_____

What are the specific connections you will ask for from your doctor, auditor, lawyer and architect?

_____
_____
_____

Professionals have very strong business connections. It is the prerogative of the entrepreneur to leverage them to give and receive business connections.

8

Strangers

Neeraj is an organizational development consultant. He helps companies to be future-ready by bringing the right changes in the company. Neeraj is an introvert and has inhibitions in talking to strangers. This particular incident happened in the year 2012. He had recently attended a networking training program. One day, he was attending an event organized by LinkedIn. During lunch, he was standing in the queue to get his lunch plate. The queue was long, and obviously, there were people in front of him and behind him with whom he could have a conversation. His heartbeat was running high, but he decided that he should start talking to strangers. He recollected everything he learnt in the networking training program and just turned back and said, "Hello." Only the first word was tough, then onwards, Neeraj was able to strike a conversation. It so happened that the stranger he was talking to runs an analytics company and his name is Saket. In the year 2012, analytics was very new to the IT world. Luckily, just the previous day, Neeraj had read a lengthy article about analytics in the business newspaper *Economic Times*. It really helped him. Neeraj was able to talk about Saket's area of interest, which is analytics. After a few minutes of the conversation, Saket asked Neeraj which analytics company he worked for. When Neeraj told him he is an organizational development consultant, Saket could not believe it, because Neeraj was able to talk about many technical and upcoming trends in the field of analytics. Then Saket requested Neeraj for a meeting where he wanted to explore using Neeraj's service for his company. Neeraj was so happy that he got a qualified lead and he also learnt how to have a conversation with a stranger.

Keshav is a startup mentor. He helps startups to grow and helps them in specific areas where they are struggling. Keshav is an extravert; he likes to talk to strangers and make new connections. One day, he was travelling from Chennai to Bangalore by train. He always reserves the executive chair car in the train, the costliest one, just to give himself a chance to network with high-net-worth individuals. On this journey, a lady was sitting next to him. She was reading a book. Keshav was observing this for 45 minutes. Then, when the lady closed the book and turned towards him, he smiled and asked, "How is the book, is it good?" That was his first sentence. Then they both talked about books, the kind of books she reads, the kind of books Keshav reads. They spoke about a few authors; what was the first book they read in their life, the current book they are reading. The conversation went on for close to 90 minutes. Then each of them took rest and again, 60 minutes before the final destination, Keshav started a conversation. Then the lady asked Keshav what he did for work. When Keshav told her he is a startup mentor, the lady introduced herself as a venture capitalist and has a portfolio of 15 startups. She requested Keshav to come and meet her and her business partner as they were looking for a startup mentor to help their portfolio startups. Keshav was so happy because this may convert into a big deal for him. He would not have got this lead if he didn't travel in that executive chair car and, more importantly, start that conversation.

Neeraj and Keshav are smart in their own way. They know that opportunities can come from anywhere. They know that leads can be generated from strangers as well.

Lead Generation During Travel

While travelling, we meet a lot of strangers. We never know who can bring a change to our life. Whenever you travel on a train, if you are an entrepreneur or sales executive, I recommend you travel in the most expensive class on that train as this would give you an opportunity to meet with high-net-worth individuals or senior executives in the industry who may be your prospective customer. If you get a qualified lead even 1 out of 10 times while travelling, it's worth it. I have personally benefitted many times from following this simple principle.

Leverage the Queue

Whenever you get a chance to stand in a queue, be happy. Because you get 2 people to network with, the person standing in front of you and the person standing behind you. The longer the queue, the better it is for you. They are going to stay with you for the next few minutes, and all you have to do is make conversation. Especially when you are standing in a queue in an airport, when you are about to board a flight. Experts say only 3 to 5% of the world's population travel in a flight in a given year. So, the person standing next to you at the airport is most probably in the top 3 or top 5 percentage of the world who can afford such travel. The probability of him or her being your customer is very high compared to a stranger in a roadside shop. Yes, you are right, that person in the airport may not be interested in having a conversation with you; they may be tired, or they simply don't want to talk to you. I agree with you, but it may not be the case with all of them, also not with all of them every single time. You can try every time, and sometimes you may start building an amazing relationship. Not only in the queue but even when somebody sits next to you on a flight, you have a few hours with them. You can use at least a few minutes to make a conversation. All you have to do is start the conversation and follow the below basic principles.

Tips to Interact with Strangers

- Be the first one to start a conversation
- Start with a smile

- Start with a question which is easy to answer for the other person
- Converse on a topic which may be of interest to the other person
- Don't introduce yourself unless you are asked
- Don't have a conversation for a very long time, unless the other person is showing interest
- Never ask questions which will be difficult for them to answer
- Never talk bad about anything
- Talk less and allow the other person to talk more
- Listen effectively and be present 100% physically and mentally
- In the end, if you feel it was a good conversation for both parties, ask for contact details, preferably an email id
- Follow up with an email and if possible, meet again in their office

Key Takeaways

- Whether you are an introvert or extravert, you can generate leads from a stranger
- Whenever you travel, be open and have a mindset to generate leads
- When you travel on a train, reserve a seat for yourself in the expensive coach
- Airports and air travel can be good places to generate leads if you have the right mindset
- Whenever you stand in a queue, leverage that to generate leads
- Follow the tips given above on how to interact with a stranger

QUESTIONS TO PONDER

What are the questions you will ask a stranger?
_____
_____
_____

How will you introduce yourself to a stranger in a short and effective manner?
_____
_____
_____

How will you close the conversation with the stranger so that they will be in touch with you?
_____
_____
_____

> Whenever you travel, if possible, give yourself a chance to interact with high-net-worth individuals by reserving a seat in the expensive travel category.

9

Newspapers and Magazines

Gopal is a designer. He makes visual communication very appealing, and he is very good at his work. This particular incident happened in the year 2011. He was reading a business newspaper and stumbled upon a news article which said a startup got 5 million dollars funding. He then searched on Google and found out the email id of the founder of that startup. He sent an email to the founder on how he could add value to that startup and also shared some of the work which he did for other clients.

After 3 days, he got an email asking him to come and meet the marketing and HR team of the startup. When he saw the email trail, he noticed the founder had forwarded his email to the respective departments and asked them whether they needed Gopal's service. Gopal met them and started doing small work for them, and within the next 5 years, that startup became one of India's poster boys in the startup world.

Vasu works as a sales manager in a reputed IT services company. He is a vivid reader, and one day he was reading a business magazine. The cover story in that magazine was about an American company, and the Global Research and Development head of this Fortune 500 company had given an interview. He talked about how for the past 10 years his company has been leveraging the talent in India and how thousands of Indian engineers are working on some of the cutting-edge technologies of his company. During his interview, he also gave the names of some of the division heads who are handling specific projects. Vasu quickly noted down the names and got around 12 names from that interview. He went to LinkedIn and got connected with all of them. Then he followed up with them for an appointment. Eight of them agreed to meet him. During his meeting, he got his company's president for the Asia Pacific, and finally, he was able to send 3 proposals and closed a deal for US 450,000. Totally, it took him around 14 months to close the deal from the date of reading that article. But that one magazine article has given him a business which is 45% of his annual sales target. He created a business deal out of a news article.

Business Newspaper

Gopal and Vasu know how to create leads from the news they read. If you are an entrepreneur or sales executive, you can generate leads through business newspapers or business magazines. Every single day, you will read news about startups getting funding, big business houses launching new projects, new manufacturing plants and their expansion plans. There are plenty of leads in business newspapers, but only very few people are able to see them. If you are a small business owner, whatever domain you are into, you can work with early-stage startups or growth-stage startups. Focus only on funded startups. The moment startups get funding, they have pressure to grow fast. Venture capitalists fund a startup only for its growth. The money startups raise has to be spent on product development or hiring people or on business growth. In simple words, it is spent on technology, people or sales and marketing. Your service can be catered to any of this. Focus on funded startups. Get connected to the founders. Connect with them on LinkedIn. Explore who among your contacts can help you in reaching out to the founders. When you meet them, give them a compelling offer on why they should work with you. Talk to them in the long term. Even if you have to do sample work for free, go ahead and do it. If you work with 10 funded startups, 1 out of it will most probably make it big. You will grow along with the company. I have seen so many of my business friends grow along with funded startups. When I was running my recruitment company, my major lead generation came from business newspapers.

Getting Leads from Business Magazines

Reading business magazines not only gives you knowledge, it also gives you a lot of leads. In most of the magazine interviews, you will get the names of the founders or business heads. Then from Google or LinkedIn, you can get their email id. Write an email to them, with specific extracts from the interview which inspired you. Ask for an appointment to meet for 10 minutes or get an appointment for a short call. Imagine if you send 2 such emails every week, in a year, you would have sent 104 such emails. I agree with you that out of 104, 90% will not reply to you. But 10% of people will reply, and you can convert 1 or 2 deals out of this. Those 2 deals will be worth a few million Indian rupees. And with your good service, you can keep getting repeat orders. Many people focus on the 90% who don't reply and don't want to do that work. Focus on the 10% which is giving you money. Try this for 1 year and based on the result you can decide whether to continue or not. You read the magazine for business knowledge and the leads you get are a bonus. The extra time you spend is to write an email. It takes a maximum of 10 minutes to write that email. In a week, that's 20 minutes and the outcome is a few million rupees. Think about this. It is a simple way that many people don't follow.

Leverage Advertisement in Newspapers and Magazines

Another way to generate leads from newspapers and magazines is to focus on the advertisements. When you see an advertisement that a particular company is recruiting a lot of engineers or managers or sales executives, then they are in growth mode. Any company which is growing may need the following services like real estate, interior design, office furniture, training, coaching, catering service, transport service, printing service and many other services to cater to the people. In that advertisement, you will see contact details; call them or email them. Again, the 90% rule will apply here. Only 10% of people are going to reply to your emails or calls. But you will get to know which are the companies that are growing. You can leverage the FRIENDS framework to connect to that particular company to get a lead.

Key Takeaways

- Read business newspapers and magazines every day
- Read them with a mindset to generate leads
- Write an email or LinkedIn message to the leads you generated from newspapers and magazines
- Make them experience your work
- Don't worry about the 90% who don't reply to you; focus on the 10% who are engaging with you
- You can generate leads from advertisements of the companies which are in growth mode

QUESTIONS TO PONDER

How much time do you spend every day on business newspapers and magazines?

_____

_____

_____

How will you generate curiosity in your first email or call so that prospective customers give you an appointment?

_____

_____

_____

Are you ready to put in efforts every week to follow the steps suggested in this chapter for the next 1 year?

_____

_____

_____

> Newspapers and magazines alone can give you enough leads to achieve your target. All we need is a mindset to find those leads when we read them.

10

Linkedin

Kishan is a business consultant specializing in operational efficiency. Till recently, he was an operations head in a manufacturing company. As this is his first entrepreneurial venture, he didn't have much of an idea about lead generation. One of his friends told him to leverage LinkedIn to generate leads. Kishan started writing articles on LinkedIn about operational efficiency. He also uploaded a video every week on a small concept related to improving efficiency. He also liked and commented on posts and articles of his prospective customers. He was doing this for close to 18 months. After 18 months, he started getting LinkedIn messages from businesspeople, asking for his expertise. After 2 years of continuous efforts on LinkedIn, now he gets 60% of his leads from LinkedIn without spending any money. He is getting leads from corporates and also from solopreneurs and individual business owners.

Kishan is smart enough to leverage LinkedIn. Can you get leads from LinkedIn without spending any money? Yes. Absolutely, it is possible. All you need is discipline, consistency and patience. First, understand whether your prospective customers are using LinkedIn or not. For most businesses, whether you are in the B2B space or B2C space, you will find many of your prospective customers are using LinkedIn. If this is true, the below activities can get you leads from LinkedIn.

Posts

Whatever business you are in, you have to keep contributing to the world in your area of expertise. I recommend you post only in the area of your expertise so that you will have a specific set of followers. Your post can be your own small message or quote or information you got from somebody. Give proper credit to the person who created that information. I recommend at least 1 or 2 posts in a week giving specific knowledge or information to your followers.

Videos

Videos grab attention. If you are good at making videos, you can share your knowledge through short videos. Don't worry about making the video highly professional. If you can make professional videos, that's well and good, but that is not mandatory. The audience looks for genuine content which adds value to them. An authentic and original message is more important than the glamour of the video. You can also share videos made by other people, giving proper credit to them. The purpose of sharing the video is to give value to your followers. At least 2 videos a month are a good start. You can increase it based on the feedback and your interest level.

Articles

If you are a subject matter expert, write articles on LinkedIn. One article a week will be a great engagement for your followers. If you are a business owner, you can write articles about what is happening in your industry. You can quote famous people, their interviews and your opinion on that matter. Give proper credit if you take information from a particular report or web page. Your personal opinion on that information is more important. Take care that the information you share is authentic and reliable.

Likes, Comments

It's not only about what you are adding but also about your visibility. Follow people who are experts in certain domains. Like their post and add specific comments; add them using @authorname so that the author of that post knows that you have given your comment. Other people who are also posting comments will see your name and they may start following you. I would recommend making 2 or 3 comments every day on other people's posts. Don't do it for the sake of doing it. Do it only if you are connected to that particular post, video or article.

Profile Page

Keep your profile page updated. It should capture all the latest things you are doing. Ideally, the profile page should be updated every month. Take care that you have a professionally shot picture on your profile page. Your background photo on the profile page should capture your expertise. This may look like a small thing, but it is your personal brand. Pictures speak a thousand words.

Connections

Search for your prospective customers and send them connection requests. If you are new to LinkedIn and have fewer connections, then I recommend you should search and send at least 10 new connection requests a day. You can reduce this once you get a few thousand connections. Don't worry about whether they will accept your connection or not. At the same time, don't send connection requests recklessly to everyone. Send it only to people with whom you want to be in touch. Also, accept connection requests from people. Before accepting it, view their profile once and then take a call.

Daily Discipline

Don't try to do all the above things in a single shot in a week. Every day, you should allocate a few minutes to LinkedIn. Whenever I am free, or if I'm waiting for somebody, I spend time on LinkedIn. Use the mobile app and keep observing what others are doing on LinkedIn. Like it, share it or comment on it based on your interest. Allocate appropriate time in a week for videos, posts, flyers or articles. Do this for 18 months and see the magic. Consistency and authenticity will definitely get you leads. All this without spending any money.

Lead Generation

Doing all the above things for 18 to 24 months will give you leads. I am quoting a very conservative period. Some of you may start getting leads from 3 months onwards; it depends on the kind of business you do and the credibility you already have in the market. But doing it for close to 2 years will most probably get you leads. The other way of getting leads is explicitly asking your prospective customers, using LinkedIn messages, for a face-to-face meeting or video meeting. To get your message, they have to be in your 1st level connection already. Hence, the first task is to get connected to your prospective customers by sending them connection requests. Once you have a sizeable number of connections, start asking for appointments. Even if 1 out of 10 such requests results in a meeting, it will be fruitful for you. Remember that today corporates are more interested in your LinkedIn profile than the profile you send to them by mail.

Key Takeaways

- You can generate leads through LinkedIn without spending any money
- Give specific knowledge or information to your followers with 1 or 2 posts a week. More the better

- A minimum of 2 videos a month will give variety to your audience
- If you write well, an article a week will be a great engagement for your followers
- Every day write a minimum of 2 or 3 comments on people's posts. It should be on different posts. Do it only if you are genuine about your comment. This will increase your visibility
- Have a good profile picture and relevant background photo on your home page
- Continuously improve your connections. If you are new to LinkedIn, this should be your priority
- Every day spend time on the above-mentioned LinkedIn activities. Daily discipline is important
- You can send specific targeted messages to your prospective clients through LinkedIn once you have enough connections

QUESTIONS TO PONDER

How many prospective customers do you have in your LinkedIn as 1st level connections?
_____
_____
_____

How much time are you spending on LinkedIn in a week?
_____
_____
_____

When was the last time you updated your LinkedIn profile?
_____
_____
_____

> In today's world, your LinkedIn activity reveals more about you than your presentation. Your prospective customer is watching your LinkedIn activity.

11

Youtube Channel

Vamsi is very passionate about teaching yoga. He was working as a yoga instructor in a wellness institute. Due to the pandemic, he lost his job. He was financially struggling to make ends meet. He understood that he had to do something which would financially help him to survive. He heard about his school friend Ramesh Sigamani doing very well in his career.

Ramesh Sigamani is a wealth advisor and founder of Bravisa Temple Tree. He has been running his wealth advisory firm for the past 10 years. When Vamsi met Ramesh Sigamani in his office, Ramesh shared with him how his YouTube channel helped in his business growth. Ramesh has been uploading videos for the past 2.5 years, and a few months back, one of his videos went viral and got 190,000 views. His channel subscriber base grew from a few hundred to 20,000+ in a matter of 40 days. Even though this one video made him popular, it was his diligent work for the past 2.5 years that has got him credibility among his subscribers. Now he has clients across the world thanks to his YouTube channel https://www.youtube.com/c/BravisaTempleTree/. Vamsi got answers on how to promote his yoga classes.

Vamsi learnt from Ramesh about the steps to create a YouTube channel and how to increase the subscriber base. Most importantly, Vamsi didn't need to invest any money to do this. His mobile phone was good enough to start this work. Whether you are in B2B business or B2C business, it makes sense to have your own YouTube channel.

Having your own YouTube channel has many advantages. Some of the major advantages are

Inbound Leads

People who see your channel and want to avail your product or service will reach out to you. It's an inbound lead. The probability of you closing a deal in an inbound lead is very high. And one good video of yours on YouTube may give you leads again and again and again. Even when some other videos of yours become popular, people will watch all your old videos and reach out to you for a specific product or service. Some of my clients get 90% of their leads only from YouTube.

Plenty of Choices to Choose

Once you become a subject matter expert in a particular field and your channel becomes popular, you will have so many inbound leads that you can choose which lead you want to work with. For many businesses, lack of leads forces them to work with projects they are not interested in. When your channel becomes popular, you will have the problem of plenty.

Key Points to Grow Your Youtube Channel

Adding value

Every video of yours should add value to your viewer. You may target a specific type of audience; that is perfectly ok. But for that particular audience, you should add value to your video. The key message, information or knowledge you want to share should be simple and clear. The audience should not strain much to understand your language or your way of communication.

Being consistent

Out of sight is out of mind. If you really want to generate leads through YouTube, then you have to be consistent in adding new videos to your channel. I recommend at least 2 videos a week. You can start with 1 video per week, and once you are used to shooting and editing videos, go for 2 videos a week. Many of the star YouTubers upload 3 to 4 good videos every week. Being consistent should not be an excuse for the lack of quality of your videos.

Relevant to current scenario

Your videos should talk about current market challenges or advances in your industry. Though the videos are watched over a period of time, the more relevant you are for that particular period of time, the more subscribers you will get. Some of your videos may be time immaterial, meaning they can be useful at any time. Catching the market trend and advising your audience on the right path will increase your credibility and viewership.

Clarity in communication

Clarity in communication is very important to grow your channel. If you make your videos in the English language, talk slowly and clearly. Use simple words. Wherever you can communicate with a picture, add pictures. View your video at least 3 times and make corrections before publishing it.

Description

Many people don't leverage the description section of the videos on their YouTube channel. Your description section should talk more about the video. It is also the place where you can market your product or service; you should give your website link, contact details and other information. Explore and visit the best YouTuber in your particular domain and see their description section. You will learn a lot from them.

Contact details

At the beginning and the end, your contact details should be visible in the video. If you prefer to give your website or email id and want to avoid your mobile number, that is perfectly fine. But you should give the option to your audience to reach out to you or your executive assistant. It is ok to repeat your contact details 2 or 3 times in a video.

Don't worry about making the video very professional in the beginning. As an entrepreneur or new business owner, you can start small with your own mobile phone and free editing software. Once you start making money, keep upgrading to professional devices and improve the quality of the video. But this should not stop you from starting your channel. Even though I am not an expert in YouTube videos yet, you can watch my YouTube channel **https://youtube.com/c/subramanianchandramouli** and get some tips from the channel. Already, I got several inbound leads through my channel. I get a new set of customers from new geographies through my YouTube channel. All this without spending any money.

Key Takeaways

- Your own YouTube channel can be a great source of lead generation
- A good YouTube channel will give you plenty of leads to choose from
- Every single video on your YouTube channel should add value to your audience
- Being consistent in creating new videos is very important to grow your YouTube channel
- Your video should talk about challenges and opportunities at that period of time
- Clarity of communication will get you more subscribers
- Leverage the description section when you upload each video
- Your contact details should be given in each video

QUESTIONS TO PONDER

Who is the expert YouTuber in your particular domain?
___
___
___

Do you have enough bandwidth to handle more business?
___
___
___

What are the first 10 topics which will add value to your prospective customers?
___
___
___

> Your own YouTube channel can bring you a new set of customers from new geographies. If you are good at video communication, a YouTube channel can continuously give you leads.

12

Seminars and Conferences

Hari is a consultant in the field of energy management and energy audit. He consults with utilities and large real estate projects where energy consumption is very high and suggests ways to conserve energy by leveraging the right energy measuring solutions. One of his primary ways of lead generation is attending seminars and conferences. In one of the seminars, he was sitting next to a person who heads the utilities division for one of the largest cities in India. Hari introduced himself, and during the break, he had coffee with this person called Padmanabhan. Hari asked him what challenges he faces as the head of utilities for a city with a population of 10 million. Padmanabhan opened up and both of them spoke for another hour; they even skipped one session of the seminar. Hari asked a few more questions and gave suggestions on a few areas where it would be easy for Padmanabhan to do his work. They both agreed that they should meet again soon for further discussion. Within the next 6 months, Hari met Padmanabhan 3 times, and he got enrolled as an advisor for the city's utility company.

Vikram runs a recruitment services company. He attended an HR conference. He had to leave the event early as he had promised his wife he would take her out for dinner. It was his 8th wedding anniversary. He felt bad that he didn't spend enough time on networking to generate any leads. When he entered the lift, there was a lady inside. She had come to the same hotel to meet one of her clients. Vikram said hi to her. She replied. They introduced themselves; her name is Preeti.

Without thinking too much, Vikram asked her what she does. She said she runs an intellectual property consulting firm. Vikram asked her what kind of companies would be a good connection for her. She was surprised and happy to hear that question, and she gave her business card to Vikram. Seeing her card, Vikram was surprised as her office is very close to his house. They both agreed to meet in person shortly. The next week, Vikram met Preeti in her office. They both spoke for close to an hour, and Vikram referred her to a few of his clients. He also liked her office complex. He was looking for an office space as well. With Preeti's recommendation to the property owner, Vikram got an office space for his company. They became good friends. In the next 3 years, Vikram got 5 clients through Preeti and she got 12 clients through Vikram.

You may think the probability of you getting such leads like Hari and Vikram from attending a seminar is very less. Actually, Hari and Vikram from the above stories followed some key principles of networking. That's how they were able to get leads. If you follow the below-mentioned basic principles of networking, the probability of you getting leads from a seminar or conference will improve drastically.

Tips to Generate Leads from a Seminar or Conference

Go early and be the last person to leave the venue

When you are one of the first persons to enter the venue, there is a high probability you will even get a chance to talk to the speaker. When you are early, there will only be very few people. Even if you don't go and talk to them, they will come and talk to you. It's an easy way of getting noticed. You are already investing time to go to the seminar, leverage it to the maximum by going 30 minutes early and be the last one to leave the venue. Many people leave as soon as the seminar or conference is over, and they miss the golden opportunity. Go and meet the speakers and congratulate them on the wonderful work they did. You never know, some of your biggest leads may come just by following this simple tip.

Ask open-ended questions

When you talk to people in a seminar or conference, ask them open-ended questions. In the above stories, both Hari and Vikram asked open-ended questions. Hari asked Padmanabhan what challenges he faces as the head of utilities. Vikram asked Preeti what kind of companies would be a good connection for her. These questions made the other person talk more. In this world, where everybody is hunting business for themselves, Hari and Vikram asked questions to understand and listen to the other person's problem.

Don't sell; create curiosity and respect

When you are at a conference, everybody is selling to others. Don't do that. Instead, create curiosity about yourself and your product or service. Earn respect by showcasing your credibility as well as your product's. But don't sell. People will remember you. Your job is to make them remember you so that within the next 2 days, when you talk to them, they should be willing to give enough time to you. In other words, by creating curiosity and gaining respect, you are ensuring that you get an appointment to meet in person or through a video meeting.

Be ready with your pitch

During the break in a seminar, if somebody shows interest and wants to know more about your product or service, you should be ready with your pitch. You cannot waste that golden opportunity. Ideally, you should have a 60-second pitch which talks about what you do, why you do, why somebody should use your product/service and your recent success story. All of this can be covered in 60 seconds. If you talk for too long, the other person will lose interest. Remember, you are in a seminar or conference, you have very little time to present yourself. People who are prepared with their 60-second short pitch are more likely to get an appointment for the next round of deeper discussion.

Tell stories

During your networking time in a conference, if somebody wants to know more about your product or service, tell them a story. People may forget facts, but they will remember your story. For example, tell them about how you implemented a project in Kerala for a customer. Along with project details, talk about the places you visited in Kerala, the different foods you had, the culture of the people of Kerala. When you form a story around your product/service details, it becomes interesting and easy for the other person to remember. It's an art. You have to master the art of storytelling.

Follow up

All the above tips will become irrelevant if you don't follow up. Your intention is not to sell but to create curiosity and respect during the seminar and conference. Within the next 48 hours, call them and fix an appointment. Meet them within a week. If you don't take that action within a week, then most probably you may not do it at all. Both Vikram and Hari did exactly that and made a good business out of the leads they generated. You can also read my book *Anybody Can Sell*. In that book, there is a separate chapter on networking skills.

There are many seminars and conferences which are free to attend. You don't need to spend any money. You can start implementing the above suggestions in these free seminars. Once you get returns from these seminars, you can invest and start attending paid seminars and conferences.

Key Takeaways

- You can generate leads without spending any money by attending seminars and conferences

- You have to follow some basic networking principles
- Go early and be the last person to leave the venue
- Ask open-ended questions
- Don't sell; create curiosity and respect
- Be ready with your pitch
- Tell stories
- Follow up

QUESTIONS TO PONDER

What kind of seminars and conferences are you planning to attend in the next 6 months?

_____
_____
_____

Are you ready with your 60-second pitch? What is your success story in the pitch?

_____
_____
_____

How will you create curiosity and respect for you and your product or service?

_____
_____
_____

Seminars and conferences can be an amazing source of lead generation. Choose the conference which your prospective customer will attend.

13

Speaking Assignments

Rohit is an innovation consultant. He helps companies to bring in innovation culture and cultivate new ideas. He also has a small team of 5 members who can execute the project. As an entrepreneur with 5 employees, he has to consistently generate leads so that all of them have enough work. Initially, Rohit used to struggle to bring enough business for his team. One day, his college friend asked him to be a part of a panel discussion on *Innovation for survival and growth*. The event happened in a 5-star hotel, and close to 200 people attended the event. Rohit did a good job of presenting his ideas. Once the panel discussion was over, when all the speakers exited the stage, close to 12 people surrounded Rohit and asked him a lot of queries about innovation. Rohit patiently answered all their queries; many of them continued the discussion even during the networking dinner. Rohit exchanged business cards. Within a week, he got a meeting request from 6 companies. They wanted to explore engaging with Rohit to bring in innovation culture in their companies. Some of the companies are very big names in the industry. From then on, Rohit makes it a point to be a speaker in many reputed events in the city. It has become his lead magnet. He automatically starts getting business and now he can choose his clients.

What brought business leads to Rohit was his ability to showcase to the world that he is an expert in a specific field. When you are a speaker, the entire focus of the audience is on you. It is, in a way, like giving a sales pitch. Even though you are not selling to any specific individual, everybody who hears your speech is judging you, your ability, at a subconscious level. When you speak well, bringing out your domain knowledge and functional knowledge, people who have challenges in that particular domain or function see you as an expert and want to take your help. The key difference is you are not selling, but they are buying your service. Rohit understood that being a speaker is a great way to get quality business leads. Below steps may help you get speaking assignments.

Steps to Get Speaking Assignments

Step 1: Be a specialist

To get speaking assignments, first, you should be a specialist in a particular field. If you are an entrepreneur, then be an industry-specific specialist or domain-specific specialist. Say, for example, you are running a software product in the retail domain, you can be a specialist talking about how IT can help small retail shops to survive and grow. If you are a company secretary or lawyer working with startups, you can be a specialist talking about compliance every startup should know. Whatever domain/functional knowledge you have, make yourself a specialist to talk about that with respect to your target customers. ***You have to own a word***. In the above example, Rohit owned the word ***innovation***. He was able to connect innovation with his target customers. The world should remember you when they hear the word you own.

Step 2: Communicate that you are a specialist

Being a specialist is not enough, you have to communicate to the world that you are a specialist. The best way to do that in today's world is to use social media. Write a blog or write an article on LinkedIn, own a YouTube channel, answer queries on Quora. You can also do all the above. Keep communicating. Do this only on the word you own. If you are a specialist in the stock market, all your articles, blog posts, videos should be about the stock market. Soon you will get your own fans and you will be identified as a specialist in the stock market. Don't stop your communication. Many of my friends became celebrities by consistently giving value and communicating on these platforms. Once you cross a tipping point, you will automatically get an invitation to be a speaker. Many event managers need good speakers. They are continuously in search of specialists like you.

Step 3: Speak well

Now that you have communicated to the world that you are a specialist, you will get speaking assignments. The next important thing is to be a better speaker. If you are not a good speaker, then you will not get further speaking assignments. Practice well. Attend public speaking workshops. Consistently improve your public speaking skill. Master the art of public speaking. This is going to be your lead magnet for your primary business. Don't forget to talk about your business during the speech and, at the end, give your contact details so that people can reach you. Promote your speaking event on your LinkedIn, Twitter, YouTube so that more people see you. Promote your social media contact details in your speech so that more people follow you. It has to go in a spiral. The speaking event should increase your social media followers and your social media followers should attend your speaking event. All this can happen only if you speak well in each event.

Step 4: Continue doing this

You should not stop this as soon as you get a few leads. You never know where it will take you.

One of my goals is to become a speaker at the World Economic Forum, Davos, Switzerland. To reach there, I should keep speaking at various forums, giving value to my audience. The more and more you speak, you will become an expert in speaking. Leads will start flowing automatically and you can choose with whom you want to work. You will become a brand for your company. Take speaking assignments at a regular frequency which is comfortable for you. For example, 2 speaking assignments in a month. This will not only help solopreneurs or consultants; even if you are running a company with 1000 employees, being a speaker will bring more leads to your company. Take care that you have a team to follow up on those leads and execute it to perfection.

Key Takeaways

- Being a speaker brings you more leads
- By being a speaker, even if you don't sell, people will buy as they see you as an expert in your field
- To become a speaker, you should be a specialist in one particular domain or function
- You should own a word
- Once you become a specialist, communicate to the world that you are a specialist
- Use social media platforms like LinkedIn, YouTube, Quora, Twitter to tell the world that you are a specialist
- Once you get speaking assignments, do it with commitment and speak well
- Continue doing this at a regular frequency and get leads without spending any money

QUESTIONS TO PONDER

What is the domain/function in which you want to be a specialist?
___
___
___

What is the ONE word you want to own?
___
___
___

How many speaking assignments can you handle in a month, and what are your plans to get those assignments?
___
___
___

> When you speak on a stage, you are a celebrity. You don't need to generate any leads; it will automatically come to you. Being a speaker is an amazing way to generate inbound leads. Inbound leads have higher probability of sales closure.

14

Testimonials

Sudarshan runs a computer sales and services company. He caters to big corporates and small businesses. If you go to his office and wait at the reception, you can see a television. You can watch the video testimonials of many of his customers from various industries. Any visitor who sits in his reception area cannot miss these few minutes of video which is well made. Sudarshan got many customers from this simple strategy. He also uploads the video to his LinkedIn, Facebook and YouTube channel. His website has the testimonials in text format. Every week, he makes a flyer testimonial and publishes it on his LinkedIn page and Facebook page. Whenever he sends a business proposal to prospective customers, he takes care that it has at least 3 or 4 testimonials from the same industry or similar industry. In his reception area, there is a file which has all the testimonials in printed form. Some of his visitors browse through the file. 40% of leads for his business comes through the testimonials' promotion.

Sudarshan follows many of the basic principles of getting testimonials and also knows how to promote them. These basic principles will help you get leads through testimonials. Before going to the basic principles, you should know why testimonials are important.

Why Testimonials Are Important

When a new prospect is exploring working with you, he or she will have apprehensions about your quality, whether you will deliver on time and many more apprehensions. Doubts are always in their mind. Genuine testimonials clear these doubts. It gives confidence to the prospective buyer that you can be trusted. Your product or service is genuine. It's social proof. Very recently, when I had a discussion with a prospective customer who runs a very big IT infrastructure company, he told me that he saw my LinkedIn activity and read the comments of my participants. That's the reason he wanted to talk to me and explore training his staff. It was an inbound lead for me. *People give more weightage to other people's words about you than what you talk about yourself.*

Different Kinds of Testimonials

Video testimonials

Today, videos are consumed more than text, and it is very easy to record a video using our smartphones. Once you have given good service to your customers, ask them for video testimonials. Tell them to give a proper introduction of themselves and their business as it is a promotion for them as well. If you have a shop and are in the B2C (Business to Consumer) segment, record a testimonial video in the shop as soon as a purchase is over. If your customer is not ready to shoot a video testimonial themselves, then offer to shoot the testimonial in their office. Your investment of time and effort will be worth it.

Audio testimonials

Some of your customers may not be comfortable with a video shoot. In that case, go for audio testimonials. Ask them to record the testimonial on their mobile phone and send it to you. You can use it as an audio file for promotion or create a text testimonial out of it.

Letterhead testimonials

Some of your customers may prefer to give the testimonial in writing. Request them to give it on their letterhead with their logo and address.

This gives more creditability to the testimonial. If your customer is happy with you, they will definitely be ready to give it in their letterhead.

Flyer testimonials

If you have more written testimonials and audio testimonials, you can get permission from your customers and, using their photo and name, you can create a beautiful flyer and promote it across your social media channels.

Testimonials from different industry verticals

A testimonial from an auto industry customer may not connect with a prospective customer from the pharma industry. Hence, try to get testimonials from different industry customers. For each industry, you should have at least 2 or 3 testimonials. Some customers would have just started their business, some may be very well established. A very well-established prospect may not be impressed with a testimonial from a startup; he would prefer to see if you have worked with a customer similar to his business size. Similarly, a startup founder would prefer to know whether you have worked with similar startups. Different verticals, different business sizes, different geographic locations are all important while receiving testimonials.

Promotion of testimonials

All the efforts to get different types of testimonials from different industries, different business size of customers will be in vain if you don't promote the testimonial. You are getting the testimonial so that prospective customers can see it. Promote it on your LinkedIn, Facebook, Twitter, YouTube, website and have a printed copy of it in your office reception. The frequency of your promotion can be 1 testimonial every week. If you have fewer testimonials, then once in 15 days. Don't worry that you are bragging about yourself to the world. Nobody else will market for you. You are not saying any lies. You are marketing genuine testimonials given by your customers. In the testimonial, take care that it mentions the benefits the customer received by using your product/service rather than them talking more about you. Your prospective customers are more interested in the benefit statement. In the above example, Sudarshan followed all these basic principles and he was able to get more leads without spending any money.

The most important thing to do is to *ask for testimonials* from your customers. Your customers are busy in their own world. Only when you ask, they will remember to give you a testimonial. Don't feel shy to ask. You have done a good job; you can confidently ask for it. To know more about how to ask, you can watch the video "Power of asking" on my YouTube channel. https://youtube.com/c/subramanianchandramouli

Key Takeaways

- Testimonials are a great way to generate leads without spending any money
- Testimonials give social proof and hence they are important for your prospective customers
- You should get video testimonials, audio testimonials and testimonials on the letterhead of your customer
- It's better to get testimonials from customers of different industries, different business sizes and different geographic locations
- Promotion of testimonials on various social media platforms and also in your office reception is very important
- To do all of the above, you should have a mindset to ask for testimonials

QUESTIONS TO PONDER

Who are the customers you are going to reach out to for testimonials?
_____
_____
_____

Do you have testimonials from customers of target industries?
_____
_____
_____

How are you planning to promote the testimonials?
_____
_____
_____

> Your prospective customers will look for social proof before they make a buying decision. Testimonials are one of the best ways of social proof.

15

Existing Customers

Mukund runs a recruitment firm. He has his office in Bangalore, India and has clients across India and the Middle East. On the 1st week of April 2016, he sent a mail to 160 of his Indian customers wishing them "Happy Financial New Year." He thanked them for their support. In India, the financial year runs from April 1st to March 31st. Out of the 160 personalized mails he sent, 124 customers replied saying thanks. Out of which, 16 of them gave him some new work. Within the next 30 days, another 8 out of the 124 gave him new orders. In that year, 18% of his business revenue came from this one mail. One of his customers replied that this was the first time somebody had wished him a *happy financial new year.*

Mukund also prepares a list of the top 25 customers every year and meets them every 6 months in person. There is no agenda. He just goes and meets them, wishes them and comes back. It's a relationship-building exercise he does every year. Within the next 4 to 6 weeks, at least 25% of those customers will give him some new work. This happens every time for him. Once, Mukund was working with a young woman entrepreneur who runs a startup. He spent so much time in getting the right technical people for her, but due to salary expectations, no positions were closed. One day, Mukund asked her whether she could refer him to some of her contacts. She understood that Mukund was not making any money with her but was still giving his best efforts, so she decided to help him. She is from one of India's premier engineering institutes and she wrote a mail to her classmates about Mukund's service and how committed he is to customer service. Anil, one of her classmates, who just started a product startup in California, saw this mail and contacted Mukund. Anil wanted to start a development centre in Bangalore. Anil became Mukund's client, and Mukund billed a million Indian rupees with Anil within the next 1 year.

In the above example, Mukund leveraged his existing customers to the fullest. Mukund understood that it may cost 5 times more to get a new customer than to get business from existing customers. You can get more business from existing customers and also get new leads from existing customers. In the above example, Mukund did both of these to perfection.

Steps to Leverage Existing Customers

Step 1: Maintain customer database

You have to maintain a proper customer database. You should have the customer name, contact number, mail address, how they got referred to you, the referral source and all the other details you can capture. You can either have a CRM (Customer Relationship Management) tool or a simple Excel sheet is enough for this. Capture data of all the customers you do business with and also all the prospects where you lost business for any reason.

Step 2: Be in their mind

Many people talk to their customers only when there is a need. When you go and meet your customers without any need, without any agenda, they will most probably like it. Just go and meet them and ask for feedback. Discuss business trends. Don't ask for any favour. You will be in their mind. When there is a need, you will be the first person they remember. They appreciate that you are the person who will be with him/her irrespective of whether there is a business need or not. Another simple way of being in their mind is to send them personalized wishes on special occasions, which many of us do. Even though everybody does that, I recommend you still do it with more creativity and care. Don't miss any opportunity to be in their mind.

Step 3: Add value to them even when there is no business

Everybody adds value to their customers. Can you add value to your prospective customers? Think about this. You have not made any money from this company, but still, you add value to them by giving them relevant domain information, competitor analysis, research reports, announcements of events relevant to them. Something useful to them. This has to be done with prospective customers where you have lost a deal. If you have sent a proposal, it means you have made a relationship. Once a relationship is made, it's your duty to nurture it. The best way to do that is by giving something useful to them. Soon they will become your customers or, more importantly, they will refer you to other businesses, and you have generated that solid lead without spending any money.

Step 4: Ask for leads

The most important part is *asking* for referrals from existing customers. By following step 1 and step 2, you will get more business from existing customers. By following step 3, you may get business from prospective customers. By following step 4, you are going to get business from new customers to whom you don't have any access. When an existing business or existing company refers you to another company, it has more value. It opens up a new set of customers for you. Prepare a list of the top 100 existing customers and ask at least 25 of them for new referrals every quarter. Even if 5 customers give you new leads every quarter, it will be a great way to get leads without spending any money. I generally ask my customers to give me just 2 referrals. Giving the number 2 makes them think only for 2 prospective names with whom I can do business. To know the power of asking and to understand the 5 magical ways of asking, you can read my book *Anybody Can Sell*.

Key Takeaways

- It takes 5 times more effort to get business from new customers than from existing customers
- You should maintain a proper customer database
- Include the database of prospective customers to whom you have sent a proposal but didn't win a deal
- Be in the customers' minds. Leverage every opportunity to interact with them
- Meet your top 25, top 50, top 100 customers in person at least once a year
- Add value to your prospective customers. They will soon become your customers
- Follow the *power of asking*. Ask for referrals from your existing customers

QUESTIONS TO PONDER

How are you maintaining your customer database?
_____
_____
_____

What are your plans to visit/e-meet your top 25 customers?
_____
_____
_____

How are you going to add value to your prospective customers with whom you didn't win a deal?
_____
_____
_____

> Smart entrepreneurs and salespeople get more business from existing customers and their referrals. It takes 5 times more effort to win a new customer.

Recommended Books for Further Reading

I recommend to my readers the following books to enhance their sales knowledge. I respect and appreciate all the authors mentioned below for contributing their knowledge to the world.

- *Positioning: The Battle for Your Mind* by Al Ries & Jack Trout
- *The 22 Immutable Laws of Marketing* by Al Ries & Jack Trout
- *Be a Sales Superstar* by Brian Tracy
- *You Can Sell: Results are rewarded, efforts aren't* by Shiv Khera
- *The Ultimate Sales Accelerator: One surprisingly powerful strategy to create EPIC sales in business and in life* by Amit Agarwal
- *Secrets of Closing the Sale* by Zig Ziglar
- *The Ultimate Sales Machine* by Chet Holmes

About the Author

Subramanian Chandramouli is the founder of Vrddhi Business Solutions. He conducts sales training and sales mentoring across many countries. He has trained more than 7500 people in various aspects of sales. He has trained 25 different nationalities that include people from India, US, UAE, Canada, Netherlands, Germany, Russia, Bangladesh, Pakistan, Sri Lanka, Afghanistan, Bhutan, Sudan, Nepal, Tunisia, Egypt, Portugal, Oman, Norway, Maldives, Malaysia, South Korea, China, Saudi Arabia and the Philippines. He does a lot of programs in the Middle East.

Some of his training programs:
- Be a Sales Super Star
- Inside Sales
- Advanced Selling Skills
- Account Management (Sales for Delivery Team)
- Customer Delight
- Negotiation Skills
- Pricing for Profit
- Interviewing Skills
- Entrepreneurial Mindset
- Sales for Startups
- Effective Channel Sales
- Negotiation Skills for Procurement Team
- Advanced Negotiation Skills
- Conflict Management
- Influencing Skills
- Building Trust
- Personal Effectiveness

- Leadership through Movies
- He is a speaker at SAARC Chamber of Commerce, IIM – Kozhikode, SP Jain
- He is a Certified **MahAcharya** Trainer. "Train the Trainer" program by **Prof. Srinivasan Ranganathan and Meena**
- Certified "Train the Trainer" of **T. Harv Eker's** Signature TTT Program
- Certified in "**SPIN Selling**" by Huthwaite Singapore

If you want to get trained by Subramanian or have paid one-to-one consulting sessions/for speaking assignments, you can reach out to him at subramanian@subbu.co

You can visit his website www.subbu.co for more details. You can follow him on Facebook at @subbusalestrainer and on LinkedIn at https://in.linkedin.com/in/subramaniancm

Annual Sales Excellence Program

Subramanian Chandramouli has a mission to transform *1 Million Entrepreneurs and Sales Executives*. One of the ways he wants to help entrepreneurs and sales executives is through his Annual Sales Excellence Program.

This program generally starts in January and July of every year and runs for 12 months. The complete program is done online. It's a live training program where participants will have a 3-hour session every month. They will also be a part of a WhatsApp group where their doubts are clarified. For one year, they are given hand-holding in their sales challenges. A total of 36 hours of live training sessions. Participants from India, Saudi Arabia and Sri Lanka are part of the current batch. If you want to join either the January or July batch, you can write an email to subramanian@subbu.co and block your seat.

www.ingramcontent.com/pod-product-compliance
Lightning Source LLC
Chambersburg PA
CBHW030839180526
45163CB00004B/1378